# Madison

# Madison

Photography by
**Brent Nicastro**

Prairie Oak
P R E S S

Madison, Wisconsin, USA

First edition, first printing
Copyright © 1999 by Brent Nicastro

Prairie Oak Press
821 Prospect Place
Madison, Wisconsin 53703 USA

Designed by Flying Fish Graphics, Blue Mounds, Wisconsin
Translations by Accuworld LLC, Chicago, Illinois
Printed in Korea

ISBN 1-879483-63-7

For Nora, who has given me support,
inspiration, understanding,
constructive criticism,
and, most of all,
her love and friendship

# Introduction

When I was fifteen my parents dragged me, kicking and screaming, from my home halfway between the Cascade Mountains and the Pacific Ocean in the beautiful state of Oregon, to this place called Wisconsin, which to my young mind was probably a Native American word meaning "one big farm." I was not pleased, and spent my first few years here trying to figure out how to escape back to the Pacific Northwest.

By the time I was old enough to strike out of my own, it was too late. I'd spent too many hours driving through the scenic Kettle Moraine Valley with the top down on my 1960 MGA and had slowly and unwittingly fallen in love with this beautiful state—farms and all.

I've lived in Madison since the summer of 1970, when I came to attend the University of Wisconsin. The Sterling Hall bombing had toned down the anti-war movement considerably, but the campus was still much like a police state with gassings and clubbings a regular occurrence. Madison didn't seem a very pretty place, then, and I rarely ventured more than a few blocks from my campus world.

The Viet Nam War ended, the protests stopped, and gradually I began to see Madison for what it is—one of the most beautiful and vibrant cities in the country. Madison has grown considerably since then and the isthmus has changed dramatically. For the past few years tall cranes have dominated the downtown area, and skyline photos I took just five years ago are now obsolete due to the addition of several large buildings—most notably the Monona Terrace Community and Convention Center. It's impossible not to be awed by that structure, and by its neighbor two blocks away, the State Capitol.

The most positive changes I've seen since coming here, however, are the initiations of events that bring people to the downtown area. The Saturday Farmers' Market, Concerts on the Square, the art fairs, and jazz on State Street have become the events that give Madison its identity and make it such a special place to live. I hope the photographs that follow will adequately express my deep affection for this fantastic city.

—Brent Nicastro

Madison skyline from Olin Park

Blick auf die Skyline von Madison vom *Olin Park* aus

Vista de Madison desde el parque Olin

麥迪遜市區建筑物的空中輪廓

Crowd circles the Capitol Square during a Saturday Farmers' Market

Menschen umringen den Kapitolsplatz während des Markts am Sonnabend

La multitud ronda la Plaza del Capitolio durante un  mercado sabatino de agricultores

州府廣場上一個星期六農貿集市上的人流

Sellers get ready for the start of a Saturday Farmers' Market

Verkäufer bereiten sich auf den Beginn des Markts vor

Los vendedores se preparan para el comienzo de un mercado sabatino de agricultores

售貨者正在農貿集市開始前做最后的準備

Produce aplenty at the Farmers' Market

Obst und Gemüse im Überfluß auf dem Markt

Productos en abundancia en el mercado de agricultores

農貿集市上的農產品丰富多樣

4

Produce stand at the Farmers' Market

Ein Gemüsestand auf dem Markt

Puesto de productos en el mercado de agricultores

農貿集市上的農產品柜台

The Capitol building, late autumn

Das Kapitol im Spätherbst

El edificio del Capitolio, a finales del otoño

晚秋的州府大廈

←※

Wildflower bouquets for sale at the Farmers' Market

Wildblumensträuβe zum Verkauf auf dem Markt

Ramilletes de flores silvestres a la venta en el mercado de agricultores

在農貿集市賣的一束束野花

Exterior detail, Capitol building

Außendetail am Kapitol

Detalle del exterior, edificio del Capitolio

州府大廈的外景

Fall color at the Capitol

Herbstfarben am Kapitol

El color del otoño en el Capitolio

州府的秋景

Assembly Chambers, State Capitol

Versammlungsräume im Kapitol

Cámaras de Asamblea, Capitolio del Estado

州議會眾議院，州府大廈


←⊬

State Senate Chambers, Capitol building

Senatskammern des Bundesstaats im Kapitol

Cámaras del Senado del Estado, en el edificio del Capitolio

州議會，州府大廈

First floor level, Capitol rotunda

Rundhalle im Erdgeschoß des Kapitols

Nivel del primer piso, rotonda del Capitolio

州府圓形大廈的一樓

Interior, Capitol dome

Innenansicht der Kuppel des Kapitols

Interior, domo del Capitolio

州府大廈的內景

*13*

Arches of the Capitol rotunda

Bögen der Rundhalle des Kapitols

Arcos de la rotonda del Capitolio

州府圓形大廈的拱頂

14

Senate Parlor, Capitol building

Empfangszimmer des Senats im Kapitol

Salón del Senado, edificio del Capitolio

議會廳，州府大廈

Blankets and quilts mark territory prior to a concert on the square

Mit Decken und Quilts werden Plätze reserviert, bevor ein Konzert auf dem Platz beginnt

Frazadas y colchas marcan el territorio, previo a un concierto en la plaza

音樂晚會前夕，廣場上用來占領位子的毯子、棉被

Crowd enjoys a concert on the Capitol lawn

Zuschauer genieβen ein Konzert auf der Wiese vor dem Kapitol

La multitud disfruta de un concierto en el césped del Capitolio

在州府廣場的草坪上欣賞音樂晚會的人群

The Capitol building at dusk.

Das Kapitol bei Abenddämmerung

El edificio del Capitolio en el crepúsculo

暮色中的州府大廈

↠→

Red and yellow tulips grace the Capitol grounds

Rote und gelbe Tulpen verzieren den Garten des Kapitols

Tulipanes rojos y amarillos adornan los suelos del Capitolio

紅、黃色的郁金香點綴著州府大地

Capitol groundskeeper hands a tulip to a passerby.

Der Gärtner des Kapitols schenkt einem Passanten eine Tulpe

El cuidador del Capitolio entrega un tulipán a un transeúnte

州府園地的園丁遞給行人一朵郁金香

The Capitol grounds in spring

Die Anlagen des Kapitols im Frühling

Los terrenos del Capitolio en primavera

州府園地的春景

Annual Art Fair on the Square

Alljährlicher Kunstmarkt auf dem Marktplatz

Feria anual de arte en la plaza

廣場上舉行的每年一度的美術品展銷會

Bicycle race around the Capitol square

Ein Fahrradrennen um den Kapitolsplatz

Carrera de bicicletas alrededor de la plaza del Capitolio

環繞州府廣場的自行車賽

North Pinckney Street in early winter, seen from the Capitol grounds

*North Pinckney* Street in den ersten Wintertagen vom Kapitol aus

La Calle North Pinckney a principios del invierno, vista desde los terrenos del Capitolio

初冬，從州府州府園地眺望平克尼北街

Madison Scouts Drum and Bugle Corps parade on the Capitol Square

Parade des Spielmannszugs der Pfadfinder auf dem Kapitolsplatz von Madison

Desfile del grupo de tambor y trompeta de los Scouts de Madison, en la Plaza del Capitolio

正在州府廣場上游行的麥迪遜童子軍鼓號方隊

(Overleaf) ↠→

Frank Lloyd Wright's Monona Terrace Community and Convention
Center at night, seen from B.B. Clarke Beach

Das *Monona Terrace Community and Convention Center* des Architekten
Frank Lloyd Wright bei Nacht, vom B.B. Clarke Beach aus gesehen

Centro de Convenciones y Comunidad de las Terrazas de Monona de
Frank Lloyd Wright, por la noche, vistos desde la playa B.B. Clarke

從 B.B 克拉克湖灘看法蘭克.羅依德.萊特的夢諾娜地壇社區和會

Monona Terrace Community and Convention Center, as seen from Lake Monona.

Das Monona Terrace Community and Convention Center, vom Monona See aus gesehen

Terrazas de la Comunidad de Monona y Centro de Convenciones, vistos desde el Lago Monona.

從夢諾娜湖中看夢諾娜地壇社區和會議中心

Interior detail, Monona Terrace

Innendetail, *Monona Terrace*

Detalle del interior, Terraza de Monona

夢諾娜地壇的內裝修細節

Jazz on State Street

Jazz auf der *State Street*

Jazz en la Calle State

州立大街上的爵士音樂

Madison Civic Center with Holiday Season trimming

Madisons *Civic Center* im Festtagsschmuck

Centro Cívico de Madison con adornos de la temporada navideña

披上節日盛裝的麥迪遜市中心

Neon entrance to the United States Courthouse

Neoneingang zum Gerichtsgebäude der Vereinigten Staaten

Entrada de neón hacia el Palacio de Justicia de los Estados Unidos

美國法院入口處的霓虹燈

Sidewalk diners on State Street

Restaurants auf dem Bürgersteig auf der *State Street*

Comensales, en la acera de la Calle State

州立大街路邊的小吃店

Madison's most unusual Bed-and-Breakfast, the Canterbury Inn

*Canterbury Inn*, Madisons einzigartiges *Bed-and-Breakfast*

El hotel "cama y desayuno" más exclusivo de Madison, el Canterbury Inn

麥迪遜最獨特的提供住宿加早餐的小旅館，坎特伯里小旅館

Mansion Hill Inn (foreground) and the Keenan House

*Mansion Hill Inn* (vorne) und das *Keenan House*

El Mansion Hill Inn (primer plano) y la Casa Keenan

麥迪遜的西爾小旅館(前院)和金南屋

Enjoying the sunset over Lake Mendota from James Madison Park

Sonnenuntergang über dem Mendota See vom *James Madison Park*

Disfrutando la puesta del sol en el Lago Mendota desde el Parque James Madison

從詹姆士麥迪遜公園看夢到她湖上的落日

Water skier on Lake Monona

Wasserskiläufer auf dem Monona See

Esquiador acuático sobre el Lago Monona

在夢諾娜湖上滑水

←‹‹ (Preceeding pages)

Sunrise on Lake Monona

Sonnenaufgang am Monona See

Amanecer en el Lago Monona

太陽從夢諾娜湖上升起

Rainbow follows the storm over Lake Monona from Yahara Park

Regenbogen nach einem Sturm über dem Monona See vom *Yahara Park* aus

El arco iris aparece tras la tormenta sobre el Lago Monona, desde el Parque Yahara

暴雨后的彩虹挂在雅海拉公園的上空

Basketball at sunset, James Madison Park

Basketball bei Sonnenuntergang, *James Madison Park*

Baloncesto a la puesta del sol, en el Parque James Madison

黃昏，在詹姆士麥迪遜公園打籃球

Fishing at sunset from the locks at Tenney Park

Fischen bei Sonnenuntergang an den Schleusen am *Tenney Park*

Pescando al ocaso desde las esclusas, en el Parque Tenney

夕陽西下時在唐尼公園的船閘上垂釣

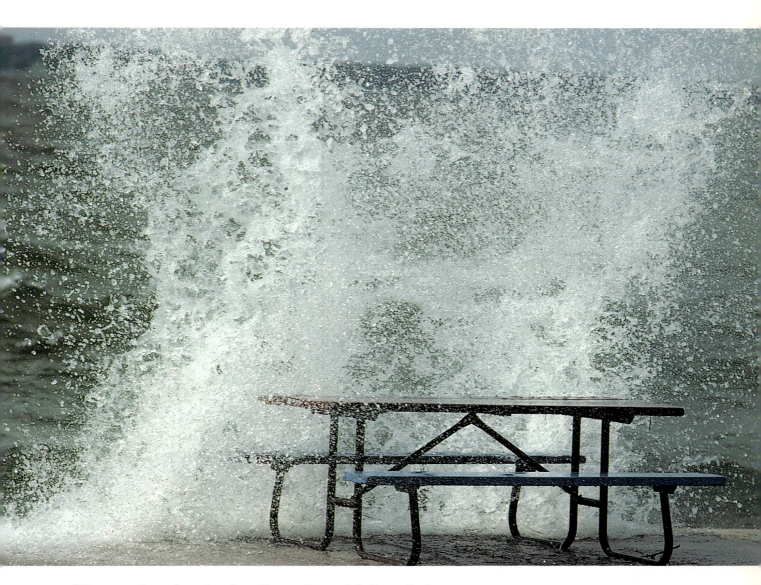

Waves crash against the shoreline at James Madison Park

Wellen brechen sich am Seeufer im *James Madison Park*

Las olas rompen contra la costa en el Parque Madison

水浪拍打著詹姆士麥迪遜公園一帶的湖濱

←K

Windsurfers on Lake Monona

Windsurfer auf dem Monona See

Windsurfistas sobre el Lago Monona

在夢諾娜湖上沖浪

43

Start of the annual Paddle & Portage race, from James Madison Park

Beginn des alljährlichen *Paddle & Portage* Rennens, vom James Madison Park aus

Inicio de la carrera anual de remo y transporte, desde el Parque James Madison

從詹姆士麥迪遜公園看每年一度的水陸賽的開始

Bike path along John Nolen Drive

Fahrradweg entlang des *John Nolens Drive*

Sendero de bicicletas a lo largo del Paseo John Nolen

沿約翰諾倫大道的自行車道

45

The Gates of Heaven Synagogue adjacent to James Madison Park

Die Tore der *Heaven Synagogue* neben dem *James Madison Park*

Sinagoga Las Puertas del Cielo ("The Gates of Heaven"), adyacente al Parque James Madison

毗鄰詹姆士麥迪遜公園的天堂之門猶太教會堂

Face painting at the annual Willy Street Fair

Gesichtsmalerei auf dem alljährlichen *Willy Street Fair*

Pintura de rostros en la feria anual de la Calle Willy

在每年一度的衛力街集會上作臉頰畫

Yahara Place Park along Lake Monona

*Yahara Place Park* entlang des Monona Sees

Parque Yahara por el Lago Monona

夢諾娜湖沿岸的雅海拉公園

Sky divers exit over East Towne Mall for a landing at Truax Field.

Fallschirmspringer springen über der *East Towne Mall* ab, um auf dem *Truax Field* zu landen

Los planeadores salen volando sobre el Centro Comercial "East Towne" para aterrizar en el campo Truax

跳傘員們离開東城商業中心，準備在喬克斯運動場降落

Skaters at the Tenney Park Lagoon

Eisläufer auf der Lagune im *Tenney Park*

Patinadores en la laguna del Parque Tenney

在唐尼公園的潟湖上滑冰的人們

←« (Preceeding pages)

Yahara River Parkway in autumn splendor

Der *Yahara River Parkway* im Herbstglanz

Bulevar "Yahara River" en el esplendor del otoño

雅海拉河公園路的絢麗秋色

Fishing through the ice on Brittingham Bay

Eisfischen an der *Brittingham Bay*

Pescando a través del hielo en la bahía de Brittingham

布雷頓灣穿冰垂釣

Ice skating family on the Tenney Park Lagoon

Eine Familie beim Eislaufen auf der Lagune im *Tenney Park*

Familia patinando sobre hielo sobre la laguna del Parque Tenney

在唐尼公園的瀉湖上滑冰的一家人

↠→

Horse and sleigh at the annual Winterfest at Monona Golf Course

Schlitten und Pferd auf dem alljährlichen Winterfest auf dem Monona Golfplatz

Caballo y trineo en el festival anual de invierno en el campo de golf de Monona

在夢諾娜高爾夫球場舉行的每年一度的冬季盛會上的馬和雪橇

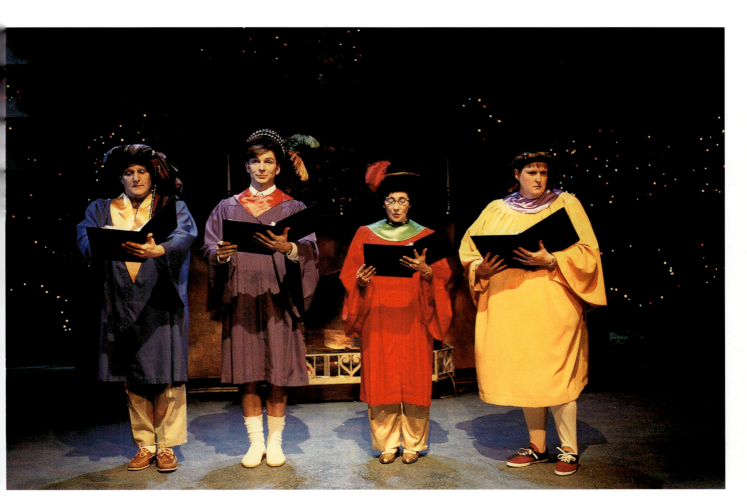

A Madison Rep performance of "Tis the Season."

Eine Madison Rep Aufführung von "Tis the Season"

Una representación en Madison de "Tis the Season" (Esta es la estación).

麥迪遜的一場 Rep 表演 "正是這個季節"

←—«

Extreme holiday decor on Jenifer Street

Üppiger Festtagsschmuck auf der *Jenifer Street*

Decorado festivo al máximo sobre la Calle Jenifer

詹妮弗街上的特別節日裝飾

57

Snowed in on Rutledge Street

Eingeschneit auf der *Rutledge Street*

Encerrado por la nieve en la Calle Rutledge

雪後的儒特樂基街

←⇤ (Preceeding pages)

Madison skyline over Lake Mendota at 20 degrees below zero

Die Skyline von Madison über dem Mendota See bei —30° Celsius

Vista de Madison sobre el Lago Mendota a 20 grados bajo cero

華氏零下二十度時，夢到她湖畔的麥迪遜市區建筑物的空中輪廓

The Rutledge Street bridge over the Yahara River in winter

Die *Rutledge Street Bridge* über den Yahara Fluß im Winter

El puente de la calle Rutledge sobre el río Yahara, en invierno

冬天，飛越雅海拉河的儒特樂基街景

Intrepid biker at the Tenney Park breakwater in early spring

Ein unerschrockener Radfahrer an den Wellenbrechern am *Tenney Park* in den ersten Frühlingstagen

Ciclista intrépido pasa el rompeolas en el parque Tenney a principios de la primavera

初春，在唐尼公園防浪堤上騎自行車的不怕冷的人

Bikers and flowering trees along the Lake Monona bike path in spring.

*Radfahrer und blühende Bäume entlang des Monona-See Radwegs im Frühling*

*Ciclistas y árboles florecientes a lo largo del sendero para bicicletas del Lago Monona, en la primavera*

春天，環繞夢諾娜湖畔的騎自行車的人們和鮮花盛開的樹

Nikki, the cat that made me a cat lover

Nikki, die Katze, die mich zum Katzenliebhaber werden ließ

Nikki, el gato que me hizo un amante de gatos

妮姬，這個讓我喜歡上貓的小東西

←⊀

Rudbeckia at the Olbrich Botanical Gardens

Rudbeckia (kornblumen) in den *Olbrich Botanical Gardens*

Rudbeckia en los jardines botánicos de Olbrich

奧伯里奇植物園的金光菊

Butterfly Garden at Olbrich

Der Schmetterlingsgarten in den *Olbrich*

Jardín de las Mariposas en Olbrich

奧伯里奇蝴蝶園

↠→

Kayaks on Lake Monona, spring

Kajaks im Frühling auf dem Monona See

Kayacs en el Lago Monona, primavera

春天，夢諾娜湖上的小舟

Pedestrian bridge over Park Street, University of Wisconsin

Fuβgängergbrücke über die *Park Street,* Universität von Wisconsin

Puente peatonal sobre Park Street, Universidad de Wisconsin

威斯康星大學公園街的步行橋

↦→

Bikers on Picnic Point

Radfahrer am *Picnic Point*

Ciclistas en Picnic Point

在野餐點的騎自行車的人們

Carillon Tower on Observatory Drive, University of Wisconsin

*Carillon Tower* auf dem *Observatory Drive*, Universität von Wisconsin

Torre del Carillón en el Paseo del Observatorio, Universidad de Wisconsin

威斯康星大學觀察大道上的卡里倫塔

Memorial Union Terrace

Terrasse der *Memorial Union*

Terraza del Unión Memorial

Memorial 學生活動中心地壇

←⊀

Flowering trees in spring on the UW Library Mall

Blühende Bäume im Frühling auf der *Library Mall* der Universität von Wisconsin

Arboles florecientes en la primavera, en la Galería de la Biblioteca de la Universidad de Wisconsin

春天，威斯康星大學圖書館附近的花樹

Outdoor exhibition of neon art on the Library Mall

Ausstellung von Neonkunst im Freien auf der *Library Mall*

Exhibición al aire libre de arte de neón en la Galería de la Biblioteca

在圖書館附近舉辦的戶外霓虹藝術燈展

A visitor admires sculpture at the Elvehjem Museum of Art, University of Wisconsin

Ein Besucher bewundert eine Skulptur im Elvehjem Kunstmuseum an der Universität von Wisconsin

Un visitante admira una escultura en el Museo de Arte de Elvehjem, Universidad de Wisconsin

一位來賓正在欣賞威斯康星大學 Elvehjem 美術館的雕塑

Students enjoy a couple of beers at the Memorial Union Rathskeller

Studenten genießen einige Gläser Bier im Rathskeller der *Memorial Union*

Estudiantes disfrutan cervezas en el Bar "Rathskeller" del Unión Memorial

學生們在 Memorial 學生活動中心的 Rathskellar 喝啤酒消遣

⇒→

UW Crew spring practice

Das Frühlingstraining der Rudermannschaft der Universität von Wisconsin

Práctica de primavera del equipo de remo de la Universidad de Wisconsin

威斯康星大學隊正在進行春季操練

Hoofers Outdoor Club sailboat on Lake Mendota at sunset

Segelboot des *Hoofers Outdoor Club* bei Sonnenuntergang auf dem Mendota See

Velero del Club Hoofers en el Lago Mendota, a la puesta del sol

暮色中在夢到她湖上揚帆的行人野外俱樂部的帆船

Hoofers sailboats lined up behind the Memorial Union at sunset

Hoofers Segeboote bei Sonnenuntergang hinter der *Memorial Union*

Veleros del Hoofers alineados detrás del Unión Memorial, a la puesta del sol

暮色中在 Memorial 學生活動中心後面排成串的行人野外俱樂部的帆船

Old Music Hall, University of Wisconsin, in autumn

*Old Music Hall*, Universität von Wisconsin im Herbst

Antigua Sala de Conciertos, Universidad de Wisconsin, en otoño

威斯康星大學老音樂大樓的秋景

UW School of Music production of Handel's "Semele"

Aufführung von Händels "Semele" des Fachbereichs Musik der Universität von Wisconsin

Producción de la Escuela de Música de Universidad de Wisconsin de "Semele" de Handel

威斯康星大學音樂學院在表演漢德爾的作品 Semele

Bikes and cars share the road on University Avenue

Fahrräder und Autos teilen sich die Straße auf der *University Avenue*

Las bicicletas y los carros comparten la calle sobre la Avenida Universidad

自行車和小車在學院大道上並駕齊驅

Science Hall, University of Wisconsin, in autumn

*Science Hall*, Universität von Wisconsin im Herbst

Salón de Ciencias, Universidad de Wisconsin, en otoño

科學大樓的秋景

Bascom Hall, University of Wisconsin, in autumn
*Bascom Hall*, Universität von Wisconsin im Herbst
Salón Bascom, Universidad de Wisconsin, en otoño
威斯康星大學老音樂大樓的秋景

The Allen Centennial Gardens, University of Wisconsin
Die *Allen Centennial Gardens* an der Universität
von Wisconsin
Los Jardines Centenarios Allen, Universidad de Wisconsin

威斯康星大學的艾倫世紀園

82

Students on Bascom Hill, in autumn

Studenten auf dem *Bascom Hill* im Herbst

Estudiantes en Bascom Hill, en otoño

秋天，在伯斯康姆山崗上的學生

UW students at the base of Bascom Hill

Studenten der Universität von Wisconsin am Fuß des *Bascom Hill*

Estudiantes de la Universidad de Wisconsin en la base de Bascom Hill

在伯斯康姆山崗下邊的威斯康星大學學生

Cheerleaders take flight at a Homecoming pep rally on Library Mall

Beim *Homecoming* bieten Cheerleader eine Akrobatikaufführung auf der *Library Mall,* um ihre Mannschaft vor dem Spiel anzufeuern.

Animadoras alzan el vuelo en un rally de resistencia, de "regreso a casa" en la Galería de la Biblioteca

正在圖書館附近進行返校節集會上表演的啦啦隊

Camp Randall Stadium filled for football

Das voll besetzte *Camp Randall* Stadion bei einem American Football Spiel

Estadio del Campo Randall lleno a causa del fútbol americano

爆滿觀看美式足球觀衆的坎普蘭代爾體育場

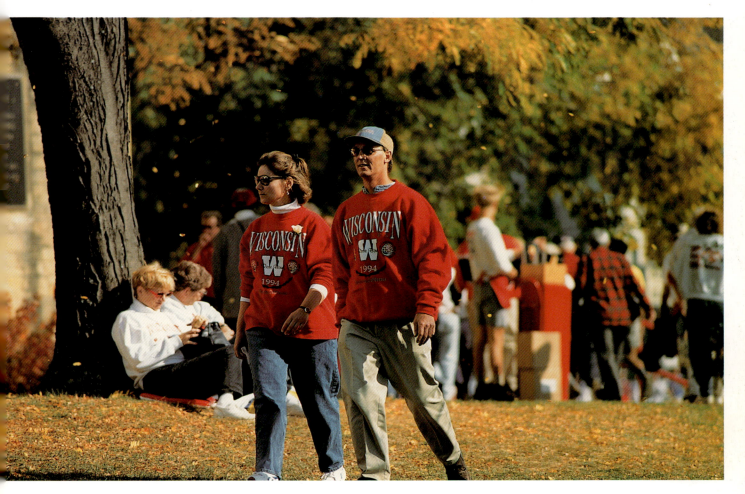

A perfect autumn football Saturday at Camp Randall

Ein idealer Herbsttag für Football im *Camp Randall* Stadion

Un sábado de otoño perfecto de fútbol americano en el Campo Randall

秋天，在坎普蘭代爾體育場的一個完美的觀看美式足球的星期六

(Following pages)

Camp Randall crowd cheers a UW touchdown

Die *Camp Randall* Fans sind begeistert nach einem Touchdown ihrer Mannschaft von der Universität von Wisconsin

Multitud del Campo Randall celebran una anotación de la Universidad de Wisconsin

坎普蘭代爾體育場內觀眾們在爲威斯康星大學隊持球觸地得分歡呼

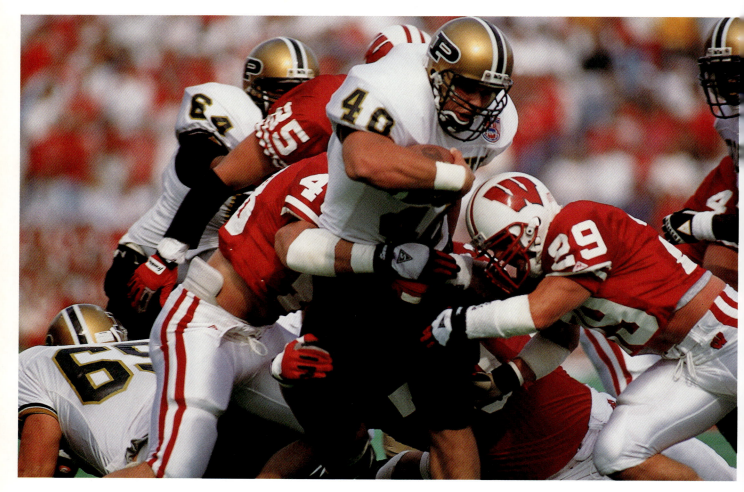

The UW defense stops a Purdue rush

Die Verteidigung der Universität von Wisconsin verhindert eine Offensive der Perdue Universität

La defensiva de la Universidad de Wisconsin detiene una carrera de Purdue

威斯康星大學隊的防守停止了普度隊的帶球進攻

Students finish a Homecoming float on Langdon Street

Studenten beenden die Arbeit an einem *Homecoming*-Wagen auf der *Langdon Street*

Estudiantes terminan un carro alegórico de "regreso a casa" en la Calle Langdon.

在蘭敦街上，學生們完成了一個返校節游車

Students on the Homecoming Court show their spirit

Studenten bekunden ihre gute Laune im *Homecoming Court*

Los estudiantes en la corte de "regreso a casa", muestran sus ánimos

返校節歡慶會上興致勃勃的學生們

Bucky Badger and students celebrate the famous 5th quarter at Camp Randall

Bucky Badger und einige Studenten feiern das berühmte fünfte Quartal im *Camp Randall* Stadion

El tejón Bucky y los estudiantes celebran el famoso 5o Trimestre en el Campo Randall

Bucky Badger 和學生們正在坎普蘭代爾體育場進行著名的賽後慶祝活動

UW Band Director Mike Leckrone

Der Direktor der Band der Universität von Wisconsin, Mike Leckrone

Mike Leckrone, el director de la banda de la Universidad de Wisconsin

威斯康星大學樂隊主任邁克.萊科隆

The trombone section moves through the Camp Randall crowd

Die Posaunisten bewegen sich durch die Menge im *Camp Randall* Stadion

La sección de trombones desfila a través de la multitud en el Campo Randall

長號隊從坎普蘭代爾體育場的人群中穿過

Law students toss canes over the goal post at Homecoming--an old tradition

Eine alte Tradition: Jurastudenten werfen Stöcke über das Tor bei der *Homecoming*-Veranstaltung

Una vieja tradición en el "regreso a casa": los estudiantes de leyes arrojan bastones sobre el poste de gol

返校節上法律學院的學生們將手杖拋過球門柱，這是一個老傳統

↠→

Memorial Union Terrace in autumn

Die Terrasse der *Memorial Union* im Herbst

La Terraza del Unión Memorial, en otoño

Memorial 學生活動中心的秋景

UW Men's basketball at the Kohl Center

Die Basketballmannschaft der Universität von Wisconsin im *Kohl Center*

Baloncesto varonil de la Universidad de Wisconsin en el Centro Kohl

科爾中心，威斯康星大學男子籃球隊

Fans begin to exit the Kohl Center after a basketball game

Nach einem Basketballspiel verlassen Fans das *Kohl Center*

Fanáticos emprenden la salida del Centro Kohl después del juego de baloncesto

籃球比賽結束後，球迷開始离開科爾中心

Sunrise on Lake Monona

Sonnenaufgang am Monona See

Amanecer en el Lago Monona

太陽從夢諾娜湖上升起

←« (Preceeding pages)

Winter comes to the Curtis Prairie in the UW Arboretum

Der Winter erreicht die *Curtis Prairie* im Arboretum der Universität von Wisconsin

El invierno llega a la Pradera Curtis en el vivero de la Universidad de Wisconsin

返校節歡慶會上興致勃勃的學生們

Brent Nicastro has been a Madison photographer for more than twenty years. He attended the University of Wisconsin and received a bachelor's degree in journalism in 1977. At that time, a strike was underway at Madison Newspapers, Inc., so Nicastro began his career as a photographer with the Madison *Press Connection*, a daily newspaper formed by the strikers. The *Press Connection* folded after two years, and Nicastro launched his freelance business, quickly becoming one of the most prolific photographers in the area. His photographs have appeared in hundreds of publications throughout the world, including *Time, People, Money, USA Today, Outside, Parade,* and in many textbooks, calendars, trade publications, and newspapers. Nicastro is a member of the American Society of Media Photographers (ASMP) and is represented internationally by Gamma Liaison in New York. He resides on Madison's east side with Nora Cusack, his wife and partner of twenty-six years, and their twenty-year old cat.